Amazing
Animal Rescue

Camilla de la Bedoyere

WOW! facts

Badger Publishing Limited
Oldmedow Road,
Hardwick Industrial Estate,
King's Lynn PE30 4JJ
Telephone: 01553 816083

www.badgerlearning.co.uk

2 4 6 8 10 9 7 5 3 1

Amazing Animal Rescue ISBN 978-1-78837-574-0

Text © Camilla de la Bedoyere

Complete work © Badger Publishing Limited 2022

Commissioning Editor: Sarah Rudd
Copyeditor: Carrie Lewis
Designer: Adam Wilmott

Page 4: Shutterstock/Pixsooz
Page 5: Shutterstock/cynoclub
Page 6: Joanne Lefson
Page 7: Joanne Lefson
Page 8: Shutterstock/Anzhelika Belyaeva
Page 9: Derek Cattani
Page 10: Shutterstock/Martin Mecnarowski
Page 11: Juliet Breese
Page 12: Shutterstock/Eric Isselee
Page 13: Shutterstock/apple2499
Page 14: Shutterstock/Colin Seddon
Page 16: Shutterstock/Tagwaran
Page 17: Shutterstock/Marian Negotei
Page 18: Shutterstock/David Tadevosian
Page 19: georgelogan.co.uk
Page 20: Shutterstock/salajean
Page 21: Alamy/Ariadne Van Zandbergen
Page 22: Shutterstock/Tory Kallman
Page 23: Alamy/Moviestore Collection Ltd
Page 24: Alamy/dpa picture alliance
Page 25: Shutterstock/stockpexel
Page 26: Shutterstock/Timothy Christianto
Page 27: Shutterstock/nurten erdal
Page 28: Shutterstock/LiteHeavy
Page 29: Shutterstock/Sergey Uryadnikov

Amazing Animal Rescue

Contents

Badger
LEARNING

1. Animals in Our World

Words **highlighted in this colour** are in the glossary on page 30

We share our planet with billions of animals. Most of them live in the wild, but we also keep many animals on farms and as pets in our homes.

Animals have rights and are protected by the law. Because animals can't speak, it's our responsibility to make sure that they are cared for and protected. Their rights include:

- access to food
- access to water
- access to shelter
- freedom from cruelty
- freedom to live their life as naturally as possible

NO CAGES NO CHAINS

LOVE CARE

CARE FOR OUR CREATURE!

ANIMALS HAVE RIGHTS TOO

NO EXCUSE FOR ANIMAL ABUSE

Speak up for us

2. Forever Homes

Animals that are kept as pets have the right to be treated properly by their owners. This means that their needs should be met but, unfortunately, this is not always the case.

REAL-LIFE STORY Lucy's Law

Lucy was a beautiful Cavalier King Charles Spaniel but she had an unhappy start to life because she lived in a tiny cage at a **puppy farm**, where she was used for breeding. Lucy suffered under terrible conditions, leading to her spine becoming damaged and some of her fur being lost.

Lisa Garner rescued Lucy, which led to her campaigning for a change in the law because she wanted to stop pets being bred in farms. In 2020, the law changed in England to ensure all dogs are born and cared for in happy homes, rather than puppy farms.

The World Woof Tour

Meet Oscar – a **plucky** pooch from South Africa who was rescued from an animal shelter just one day before he was due to be put down.

In 2009, Oscar and his new owner, Joanne Lefson, set off on a trip around the world to inspire people to adopt a dog from their local animal shelter. Oscar and Joanne visited an amazing 42 countries across five continents. The trip was named the World Woof Tour.

The Great Wall of China

The Great Pyramids of Giza, Egypt

Las Vegas, Nevada

Machu Picchu, Peru

Table Mountain, South Africa

Masai Mara Reserve, Kenya

Hollywood, Los Angeles

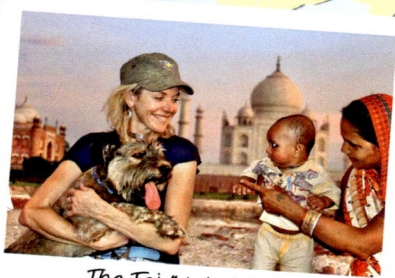

The Taj Mahal, India

3. Return to the Wild

Wild animals belong in their natural habitats, where the conditions are best for them. However, sometimes animals have to leave, or are removed, causing them to suffer.

When housing developments spread out into animal habitats, they cause damage and can even totally destroy them. This can force animals into areas where survival is difficult, which can lead to **extinction** of a species. Wild animals can be killed for their parts, such as horns or skin, and they can even be taken as exotic pets.

WOW! facts

There are about 475 million homeless dogs in the world. Some of these dogs are considered wild.

8

In 1969, Christian the lion **cub** was on sale at Harrods, a glamourous department store in London. John Rendall and Ace Bourke saw him in the shop window and immediately fell in love with him.

John and Ace bought Christian for 250 guineas, over £3000 in today's money, and took him home to their flat in Chelsea. They looked after him well, but they knew the lion could not stay as Christian was growing into a huge and powerful animal.

Wildlife conservationists advised that Christian be sent to what would have been his natural habitat, the African plains in Kenya. Releasing Christian into the wild was a success and it is thought he went on to start his own **pride**.

A lone wolf

Wild wolves once lived freely in many parts of the Unites States of America until, sadly, humans hunted them to near extinction.

Scientists wanted to understand the wolf species better in order to help them survive. In 2011 they fitted some wolves with **radio transmitters** to track them.

The scientists named one wolf OR-7 and they tracked him during a long, cold winter. OR-7 travelled 1900 kilometres to California, where wolves had not been seen for 90 years!

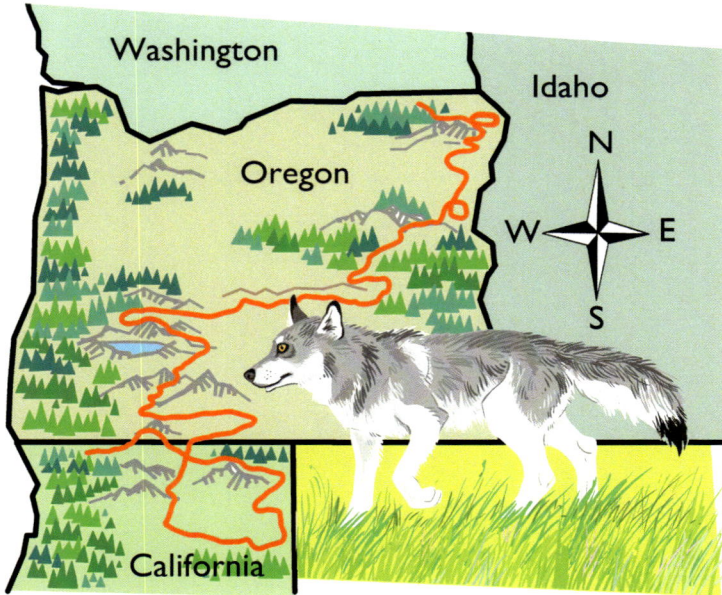

The scientists shared the details of this remarkable journey and soon many people were following OR-7's story. People began to welcome and support wolves, impressed by the incredibly long migrations they had to make in order to survive.

OR-7 eventually found a mate and started a family, which, in time, grew to become a wolf pack.

WOW! facts

Fifty years ago, grey wolves were in danger of going extinct in the USA. Now there are more than 12,000 wild wolves.

Apes in danger

The jungle in Borneo is home to the rare orang-utan. These playful apes spend most of their time living in trees, gripping the branches with their hook-shaped hands and feet.

Orang-utans are critically endangered and there is a strong chance they will soon become extinct. Their numbers are falling because their rainforest habitat is being cut down to grow trees for palm oil plantations.

Palm oil is mostly used for food and cooking, but it is also used in make-up, shampoo, and soap. Every year it is estimated that between 1000 and 5000 orang-utans are killed due to the palm oil industry.

WOW! facts

Orang-utan means 'person of the forest'.

Orang-utan orphanage

Some lucky orang-utans are rescued and taken to a care centre, or an orphanage, where they are looked after by conservation workers. The staff have to teach the babies survival skills, such as how to climb safely, find their own food and make night nests in the trees.

When the orang-utan babies have learned all the skills they need to survive, they are returned to the rainforest. They live in special areas called reserves, where they are kept safe, they live a natural life and their habitat is protected.

WOW! facts

In the last 120 years the number of orang-utans has fallen by 97 per cent.

4. Animal Farms

Humans have been farming animals for thousands of years. Modern intensive farming does not allow animals to live naturally, and they can be subjected to a lot of pain and suffering. Sometimes, farm animals can be rescued from these awful conditions and given new homes, where they can live freely.

Hen rescue

Hens are kept on farms to lay eggs but when they get too old they are slaughtered, unless someone offers to adopt them.

Caged birds often lose their feathers. A hen's feathers will regrow when she is in a happy home.

Farms around the world

About 70 billion farm animals are kept for food each year. Two-thirds of them are kept in factory farms where they live in unnatural conditions, such as indoors and in cages. People who object to this choose to eat free-range animal products, or not to eat animal products at all.

Every year:

- 6.5 billion hens are kept for their eggs
- 50 billion hens are killed for meat
- 1.3 billion pigs are killed for meat
- 250 million cows are kept for their milk
- 325 million cows are killed for meat

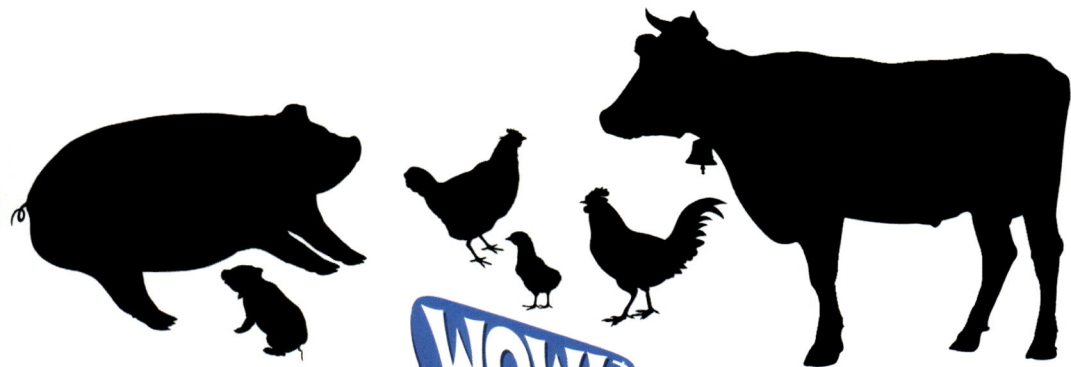

WOW! facts

The average person in a developed country, who is not vegetarian or vegan, will consume 7000 animals in their lifetime.

Bear farms

In China and Vietnam, bears are kept in cages on farms, where a liquid called bile is removed from their body and used in medicines. The cages are so small that the bears cannot move and suffer great pain when the bile is taken from their body.

The bears are often hungry, thirsty, and sick and can live in these awful conditions for up to 30 years. There are other ways to make medicines without using bear bile, but this cruel way of farming is still happening.

WOW! facts

About 10,000 bears are still farmed in Asia.

Caring for bears

Sometimes, bears can be rescued from these barbaric farms and taken to bear **sanctuaries**. They have dens for sleeping and plenty of outdoor space to walk, climb and play. They are given toys and their food is hidden so they have to hunt for it, just as they would in the wild.

A better future?

Bear farming is illegal in most countries and the practice is recognised as cruel. Charities have opened up new sanctuaries to take in more bears as the bile farms shut down due to reduced demand. Public awareness of this issue has grown and people are more interested in bear **conservation**.

5. Animals at Work

All over the world, animals are put to work. They are used to carry heavy loads and pull carts, and sometimes forced to perform in circuses or aquariums. Working animals are not always looked after and many of them need to be rescued from their unhappy lives.

Circus animals

Circus animals are kept in small cages when they travel from town to town and are made to do tricks that are unnatural and cruel. Circus animals have to perform in front of crowds, with loud noises and bright lights, which causes them to feel stressed.

Wild animals such as lions, bears, tigers and elephants can still be seen working in circuses today.

Simba the lion was only a cub when he was forced to work in a French circus. In 2014, when he was nine years old, Simba was rescued by the Born Free Foundation. He was sent to an animal sanctuary in Africa, where he could live a life as natural as possible.

The Born Free Foundation is a charity that is passionate about wild animal welfare. This is part of its mission statement:

We work tirelessly so all wild animals are treated with compassion and respect and are able to live their lives according to their needs. We oppose the exploitation of wild animals in captivity and campaign to keep them where they belong – in the wild.

Beasts of burden

Animals that are used to carry heavy loads, or to pull carts and farm equipment are called beasts of burden. The work is hard and tiring, and they are worked until they are too old or injured.

Beasts of burden from around the world include:

- buffalo
- camels
- donkeys

- elephants
- horses
- mules

- oxen
- reindeer
- yaks

WOW! facts

Over 16 million animals were put to work in World War One. Unfortunately, nine million of those animals tragically died.

Donkey work

Donkeys and mules are some of the world's hardest working animals. They are used to carry people and heavy goods, often for long distances or up steep hills. Unfortunately, donkeys are often uncared for, exploited and abused.

The donkeys of Lamu

Lamu is an island town in Africa where there are no cars or vans, so the island's 3000 donkeys do all the heavy carrying. For more than 30 years, volunteers have rescued donkeys that are suffering and worked with donkey owners to improve conditions. They make sure the animals have water to drink in the town, and shade to escape from the hot African sun. They even help to design better harnesses so the donkeys can avoid injury and feel more comfortable whilst working.

Keiko the killer whale

In 1979, a young killer whale, also known as an orca, was taken from his family in the cold waters around Iceland. He was named Keiko and he spent the next ten years alone in a small tank at an amusement park in Mexico.

In 1993, Keiko was picked to perform in a film called *Free Willy*. The film tells the story of a boy who makes friends with a captive orca and sets him free. Keiko became a star and many people wanted to help him live free, just like Willy in the film.

Keiko was given his freedom and taken back to the seas around Iceland. The scientists used radio transmitters to follow Keiko as he attempted to hunt fish and join a new orca family.

Sadly, Keiko couldn't learn how to live in the wild. He wasn't able to join a new orca family and he followed boats so he could continue to be in the company of humans. Keiko died from an infection in 2003.

WOW! facts

Around the world, more than 2000 dolphins and 60 orcas are kept to entertain people.

6. Danger!

Fires, floods and earthquakes are natural disasters that can happen without warning and are not only dangerous for humans but animals too.

Flood!

In 2021, after days of heavy rain, terrible floods hit Germany and people had to leave their homes in a rush, leaving many animals behind.

One German animal rescue service saved more than 1600 animals. They needed specialist equipment, such as boats, off-road cars, dry-suits and floating pet boxes, to help them track down and transport the animals to safety.

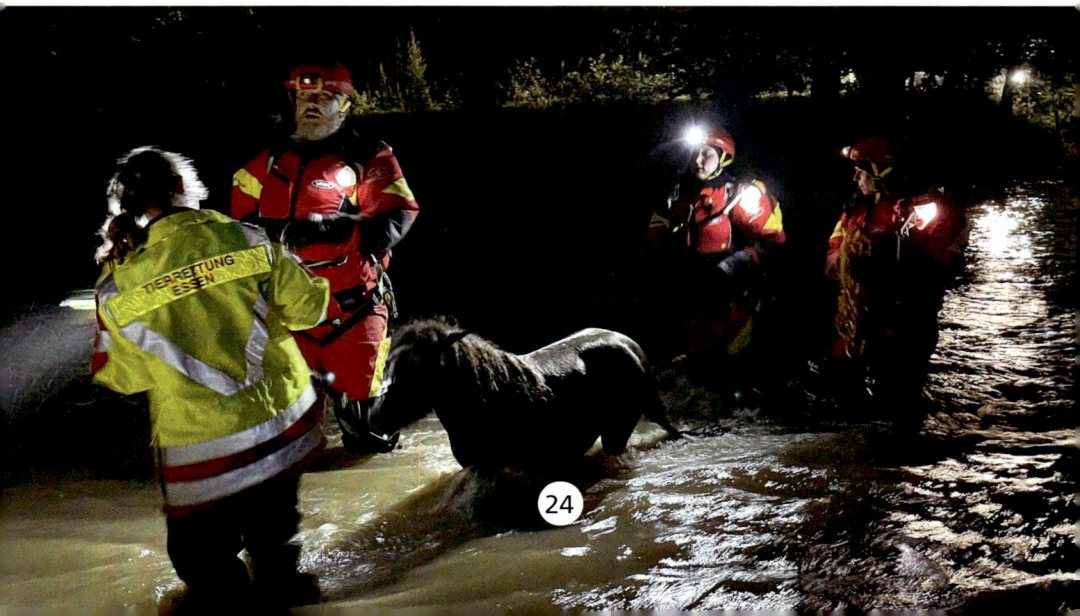

Fire!

In the summer of 2020, wildfires hit Australia which destroyed over 3000 buildings and 35 million acres of land. More than 30 people died and three billion animals lost their homes.

As the fires spread, people battled to save wildlife and care for the animals that had been left injured and homeless. When the fires began to die down, amazing tales of animal rescues began to come out in the news.

Hissy is a brushtail possum who was one of the many wild animals rescued from fires in Australia. His four paws had suffered serious burns and he had open wounds that were dirty from walking through the ash and debris caused by the fire.

Dr Carrie Hawthorn cared for his wounds every day, but they were so painful that Hissy had to be **anaesthetised** during the cleaning for the first few weeks.

Thankfully, Hissy recovered well and, once his wounds had healed, he was returned to the wild.

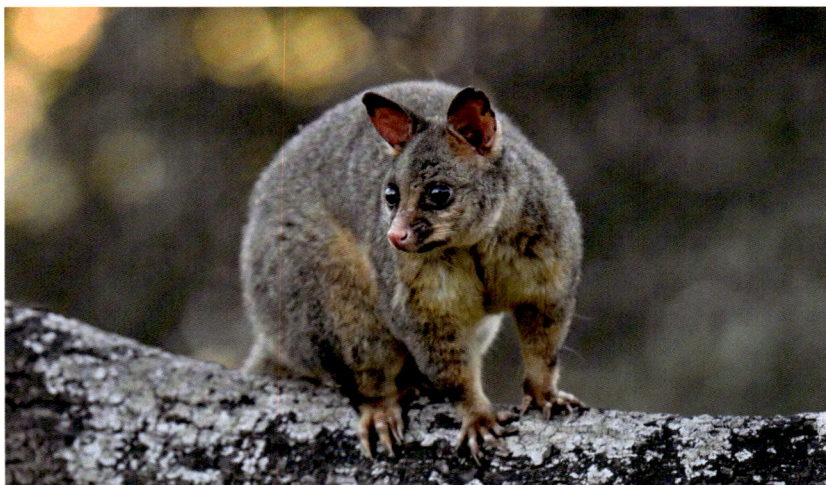

Bob the hero

In 2020, a terrible earthquake hit Turkey causing many buildings to fall down, trapping people and animals alike.

Bob, a search-and-rescue dog, was soon put to work, sniffing in the wreckage for signs of life under the rubble. He alerted the human rescuers that he had found something, and they began to remove the debris. After 29 hours, a trembling cat was pulled from the remains of the building, completely fine.

The cat was named 'Umut', which means 'hope' in Turkish, and Bob was called a hero!

Plucky penguin

Juan Salvado was a penguin who enchanted everyone who met him. Juan was facing death when a kind stranger rescued him, and gave him a whole new life.

Juan's amazing story began in the sea around South America, when oil spilled from a boat, covering hundreds of penguins in oil and tar. Many of them died, but Juan was saved by a young teacher, called Tom Michell.

Tom cleaned Juan and put him back in the sea, but Juan refused to leave Tom's side.

Tom had to take Juan back to the school where he taught. The students there loved the little penguin and they swam with him in the swimming pool.

Juan became best friends with a boy called Diego, who was sad and homesick, and generally struggling with school life. Diego began to join Juan in the school pool, and he quickly discovered that he had a talent for swimming. Diego went on to win many galas and broke all the school swimming records.

In this story of amazing animal rescue, Tom had rescued Juan and Juan had rescued Diego!

GLOSSARY

anaesthetised — to make unconscious through drugs

conservation — protecting our environments and the wildlife that lives in it

cub — the babies of meat-eating animals

extinct — no longer exists

plucky — to be brave during difficult events

pride — the name for a group of lions

puppy farm — a place of intensive dog breeding which does not care for the animals correctly

radio transmitter — an electronic device that gives off radio waves and can be used to track animals

sanctuary — a place of safety that is away from danger

wildfire — a large and destructive type of fire that spreads through woodland

Questions

What breed was Lucy the dog? *(page 5)*

Which two men bought Christian the lion from a pet shop in London? *(page 9)*

How far did the radio transmitter show OR-7 had travelled? *(page 11)*

By what percentage has the orang-utan population fallen by over the last 120 years? *(page 13)*

What was the name of the killer whale who starred in Free Willy? *(page 22)*

How many animals lost their homes in the 2020 Australian wildfires? *(page 25)*

INDEX